Goose berry Patch ™

tHe Country Friends Collection ℠

Herbs

Mary Elizabeth
... has a definite green thumb when it comes to herbs.

Holly
... is particularly fond of bee balm.

Kate
... has an Uncle Herb and an Aunt Bea.

Herbs

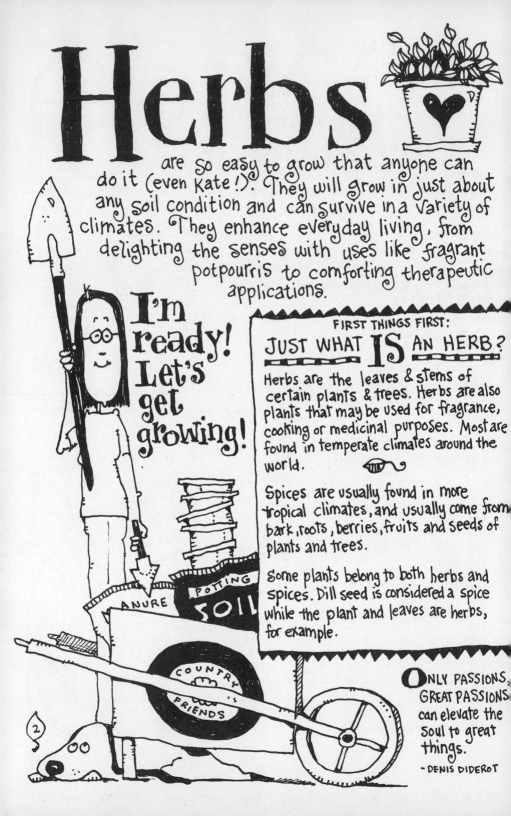

are so easy to grow that anyone can do it (even Kate!). They will grow in just about any soil condition and can survive in a variety of climates. They enhance everyday living, from delighting the senses with uses like fragrant potpourris to comforting therapeutic applications.

I'm ready! Let's get growing!

FIRST THINGS FIRST:
JUST WHAT IS AN HERB?

Herbs are the leaves & stems of certain plants & trees. Herbs are also plants that may be used for fragrance, cooking or medicinal purposes. Most are found in temperate climates around the world.

Spices are usually found in more tropical climates, and usually come from bark, roots, berries, fruits and seeds of plants and trees.

Some plants belong to both herbs and spices. Dill seed is considered a spice while the plant and leaves are herbs, for example.

ONLY PASSIONS, GREAT PASSIONS can elevate the soul to great things.
– DENIS DIDEROT

MANURE

POTTING SOIL

COUNTRY FRIENDS

2

You say "ERB" and I say "HERB"

Which is correct ?

Depends on which side of the Big Pond you live on. In America, the H is dropped from the word Herb. In England, the word Herb is pronounced with the H sound.

What was Paradise

but a garden, an orchard of trees and herbs, full of pleasure and nothing there but delights.

- QUOTE BY WILLIAM LAWSON

Keeping Your Herbs HAPPY

PROVIDE LOTS OF **SUNSHINE.** Herbs need at least **6** Hours of sun.

GIVE THEM PROTECTION FROM COLD WINTER **WIND.** FENCING & SHRUBBERY HELPS.

Good DRAINAGE

IS IMPORTANT WITHOUT IT, WATER WILL SIT AROUND THE HERB'S ROOTS & STUNT ITS GROWTH. A QUICK EXPERIMENT LIKE THIS ONE WILL DETERMINE IF YOU HAVE A PROBLEM: DIG A HOLE ABOUT 1 FOOT DEEP. FILL IT WITH WATER AND ALLOW TO SETTLE OVERNIGHT. IF THERE IS STILL WATER STANDING IN THE HOLE THE NEXT MORNING... YOU HAVE A DRAINAGE PROBLEM! ADD ORGANIC MATERIAL, COMPOST OR PEAT MOSS TO CORRECT IT.

SOIL

THAT IS NEUTRAL OR SLIGHTLY ALKALINE IS PREFERRED BY HERBS. IF YOU'RE THE DO-IT-YOURSELF-TYPE, VISIT YOUR LOCAL GARDEN SHOP FOR A SOIL TEST KIT. YOU CAN ALSO SEND A SOIL SAMPLE TO YOUR COMMUNITY'S AGRICULTURE EXTENSION SERVICE. A GOOD pH READING FOR HERBS WOULD BE pH 6 TO pH 7.

(4)

A COUNTRY FRIENDS HERBAL TIP FROM MARY ELIZABETH:

Always speak softly in a sweet tone to your herbs. Do not shout. Smile. Address them kindly.

DEAREST SNOOKUMS... MY LITTLE SWEET HEART...

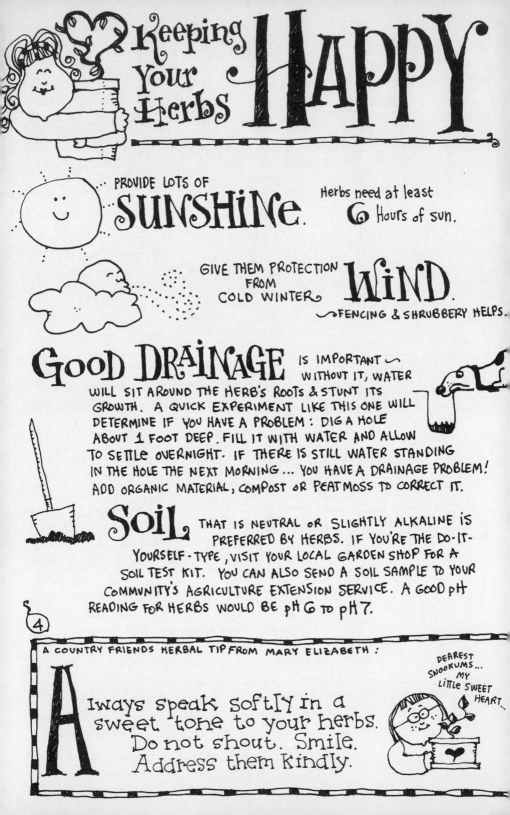

GOOD NEIGHBOR HERBS

Some herbs and vegetables make great neighbors ... and some don't!

BASIL
ENHANCES FLAVOR OF TOMATOES, ASPARAGUS & LETTUCE. REPELS FLIES... A WONDERFUL PATIO BUG REPELLENT!

BORAGE
HELPS REPEL TOMATO WORMS. BEES LOVE IT ~ EVERY GARDEN NEEDS A BUNCH OF BEES SINCE THEY ARE NATURE'S NATURAL POLLINATORS.

CHIVES
CHASE APHIDS FROM CARROTS & TOMATOES.

DILL
PLANT NEAR CABBAGE FOR GROWTH & GREAT TASTE, BUT KEEP IT FAR AWAY FROM CARROTS and TOMATOES.

GARLIC
REPELS JAPANESE BEETLES & APHIDS. LETTUCE & PARSNIPS BENEFIT FROM BEING PLANTED NEAR A FRIENDLY GARLIC PLANT.

MINT
WILL SEND WHITE CABBAGE MOTHS FLYING, SO PLANT NEAR CABBAGES & TOMATOES. MINT WILL TAKE OVER A GARDEN PLOT, THOUGH, IF YOU DO NOT KEEP IT CONTAINED ~ NOT VERY NEIGHBORLY!

OREGANO
and BEANS GO HAND-IN-HAND! JACK MUST HAVE THROWN A HANDFUL OF OREGANO IN WITH HIS MAGIC BEANS. BEES & BUTTERFLIES LOVE OREGANO, TOO.

PARSLEY
PLANT NEAR CORN, TOMATO & ASPARAGUS FOR GOOD FLAVOR & GROWTH. ASPARAGUS BEETLES RUN AWAY FROM PARSLEY.

ROSEMARY
is A GOOD FRIEND TO CARROTS, CABBAGE & BEANS AS IT DRIVES AWAY ALL KINDS OF DREADED BEETLES & BUGS.

SAGE
SAYS "SEE YA LATER" TO CARROT FLIES & CABBAGE MOTHS. CUCUMBERS & SAGE DO NOT GET ALONG!

SUMMER SAVORY
IS EXCELLENT PAIRED WITH BEANS IN THE GARDEN... A MATCH MADE IN HEAVEN.

THYME
··· BELOVED BY BEES & BUTTERFLIES, THYME STIMULATES GROWTH IN THE GARDEN.

So many to

Love MOIST CONDITIONS

CULINARY HERBS

Shade Lovers

Angelica
Bee Balm
Borage
Chervil
Chives
French Tarragon
Lemon Balm
Mint
Parsley
Sweet Cicely
Sweet Woodruff

Love Moist Conditions

Angelica
Calendula
Horsetail
Lady's-Mantle
Lovage
Mint
Parsley
Sorrel
Sweet Woodruff
Violets

Culinary Herbs

Basil
Chervil
Chives
Dill
Fennel
Garlic
Greek Oregano
Lemon Balm
Lemon Thyme
Marjoram
Mint (PEPPERMINT & SPEARMINT)
Parsley
Rosemary
Sage
Savory
Tarragon
Thyme

...To cheer the heart and Delight the senses

SWEET CICELY

...lovely in the garden with its feathery leaves, this herb has a charming name and a sweet taste.

Lady's Mantle

...has downy, rounded leaves that look as if cut with a tiny pair of pinking shears. A very astringent plant, and used to be thought to cure "women's complaints."

choose from!

DROUGHT TOLERANT – DRY SOIL

Borage
Chamomile
Chives
Fennel
Feverfew
Lavender
Marjoram
Oregano
Rosemary
Russian Sage
Santolina
Savory
Thyme

SCENTED HERBS

Chamomile
Creeping Santolina
Dill
Hyssop
Lavender
Lemon Balm
Lemon Verbena
Peppermint
Pineapple Sage
Rosemary
Scented Geranium
Thyme
Sweet Violet

INDOOR GARDENS

Basil
Chives
Dill
Lemon Balm
Marjoram
Mint
Oregano
Parsley
Rosemary
Sage
Scented Geranium
Savory
Tarragon
Thyme

⁊

CHAMOMILE

"MATRICARIA RECUTITA"

...a forerunner of lawn grass, chamomile was called "Earth Apple" by the Greeks due to its fruity scent. A popular remedy for sleeplessness, our ancestors considered it an indispensable garden herb.

DILL

...its name comes from the old Norse word, dilla, which means to lull. It is a remedy for indigestion, flatulence and is soothing to fussy babies.

In the name of the bee, and of the butterfly, and of the breeze, Amen. EMILY DICKINSON

GARDEN DESIGNS

WAGON WHEEL

EARLY AMERICAN SETTLERS WOULD USE A WHEEL OR ITS SPOKES TO LAY OUT AN HERB GARDEN. IMBED IT INTO THE GROUND HALF-WAY AND FILL EVERY SPOKED AREA WITH AN HERB.

CIRCLE GARDEN

OFTEN HAS A FOCAL POINT IN THE CENTER, SUCH AS A SUNDIAL, BIRDHOUSE OR BIRD BATH, OR A STATUE. A CIRCLE GARDEN MAY ALSO HAVE SEVERAL PATHS RADIATING FROM ITS CENTER. HERBS ARE PLANTED IN A CIRCLE AROUND THE BASE OF THE FOCAL POINT. IT SOMETIMES HAS A CIRCULAR GRAVEL PATH AROUND IT.

garden plan

LADDER GARDEN

WHAT COULD BE SIMPLER? JUST LAY AN OLD WOODEN LADDER ON PREPARED GROUND & PLANT EACH SECTION WITH A DIFFERENT KIND OF HERB!

easy!

Some TALL growing Herbs:

ANGELICA • CLARY SAGE • DILL • EVENING PRIMROSE • FENNEL • FOXGLOVE • LOVAGE • MARSHMALLOW • TANSY

8

YOU CAN DO

ROCK WALL GARDEN

·· PERFECT FOR A HILLSIDE AREA! THE WALL IS MADE OF ROCKS PUT TOGETHER WITHOUT MORTAR. OFTEN THE ROCKS ARE SUNK INTO THE GROUND TO KEEP THEM IN PLACE. FILL EMPTY POTS BETWEEN ROCKS WITH GOOD QUALITY SOIL, PACKED TIGHTLY TO REMOVE AIR POCKETS. PLANT WELL-ESTABLISHED HERBS INTO THE DIRT-FILLED SPACES ⌣ CREEPING PLANTS LOOK WONDERFUL!

Herbs WITH Evergreen Foliage:

- ·ALOE · BAY · CHERVIL · FEVERFEW · HOUSELEEK ·
- · HYSSOP · ROSEMARY · RUE · SAGE · SOUTHERNWOOD

Herbs THAT DO WELL IN POTS:

- · BASIL · BAY · CHERVIL · CHIVES · LEMON BALM
- · MINT · NASTURTIUM · PARSLEY · TARRAGON
- · THYME · SUMMER SAVORY

RAISED BEDS

HERBS THRIVE IN A RAISED BED! REMOVE GRASS, WEEDS AND A COUPLE OF INCHES OF SOIL FROM THE AREA WHERE YOUR GARDEN WILL BE PLACED. BUILD A BOX USING BOARDS, BRICKS, LANDSCAPE TIMBERS, CEDAR POSTS OR THE LIKE OVER THAT SPOT. FILL THE BOX WITH QUALITY SOIL ⌣ THEN PLANT AWAY! IF YOU HAVE A SOIL DRAINAGE DILEMMA, A RAISED BED MIGHT JUST BE THE ANSWER.

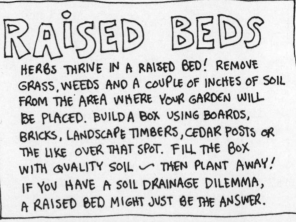

Some Creeping Herbs:

- · WILD THYME · GROUND IVY
- · CHAMOMILE · PENNYROYAL

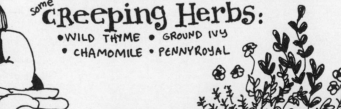

LOW-growing HERBS: SOME VARIETIES OF...

CATMINT · GERMANDER · HYSSOP · LAVENDER · ROSEMARY · SAGE · SANTOLINA · SOUTHERNWOOD · PARSLEY · THYME · VIOLETS · PENNYROYAL · PINKS · LADY'S MANTLE · MARJORAM · FEVERFEW · ADJUGA

grow an Herbal Container Garden

No room for a big garden?
Living in an apartment?
The solution is container
gardening!

Many herbs and veggies grow
well in clay pots, window boxes
or wooden tubs. Place these
containers full of herbs known
for their fragrance or
ability to deter bugs
on patios and decks.

Shallow pots are perfect for
creeping herbs (thyme, oregano
or marjoram)....

Deep pots work well for
herbs with bulb-type roots
(onions, for example)....

Shrubby or tree-like herbs
fare better in large wooden
tubs.

Life begins the day you start a garden.
-CHINESE PROVERB

KATE'S TIPS FOR A THRIVING CONTAINER GARDEN

YOU GOTTA HAVE GOOD DRAINAGE IN YOUR POTS! TRY THESE IDEAS ~

Drill holes in the bottom of wooden tubs, and make sure clay pots have holes in the bottom. Put an inch or 2 of gravel in the bottom....

...or try aluminum cans in place of the gravel. Punch holes in 'em to make sure they'll drain. Cans are very light-weight ~ large pots can be moved easily with cans in the base.

Black plastic pipes can be placed in the center of large or tall containers. Fill in with soil around the outside of the pipe, leaving center empty. Pour water into pipe when your plants are thirsty.

holes ↓

It is a good idea to provide a little mild or diluted liquid fertilizer to herbs in containers.

BIG & STRONG FERTILIZE

STRAWBERRY POTS

don't always have to hold strawberry plants .... they make wonderful containers for herb gardens, allowing you to grow a variety of plants in a small space.

Strawberry jars and clay pots should be soaked in

WATER

just prior to filling with potting soil. That way, when watering newly planted herbs, their roots can absorb the moisture, not the pot.

FOR BUSHIER, THICKER HERB PLANTS ~
PICK THEM OFTEN.

Harvesting and

Storing Herbs

Most culinary herbs reach their peak flavor just as the flower buds begin to open. Once the herbs begin to flower, the leaves become more woody or fibrous and their flavor is not as intense.

Gather herbs in the morning after the sun has dried off the dew. Late afternoon gathering is not recommended as the day's heat robs the leaves of their essential oil and color. Up to one-third of the plant may be gathered at a time ~ more than that will weaken the plant.

Never use any Herbs WHicH Have been SPRAYeD.

LIKEWISE, NEVER USE ANY FLOWER OR HERB FOR FOOD ~ EVEN GARNISH ~ UNLESS YOU'RE SURE IT'S EDIBLE!

Freezing:

For some herbs, this is the next best thing to fresh. Some herbs like sage, basil and tarragon will need to have the tough stems removed, while dill and thyme freeze well left in sprigs. Basil freezes better if blanched before freezing ~ otherwise, the nice green leaves turn black. Simply pour boiling water over leaves in a strainer for one or two seconds. Lay leaves on paper towels to dry and cool before freezing.

For soups and stews, try mincing or puréeing herbs (1 T. water to 1 T. herbs) and freezing in ice cube trays. Store in plastic bags until needed.

HERB

Drying Herbs:

★ DRYING SCREENS

Layer clean dry leaves on a fine-mesh window screen. Be careful not to crowd them. Screens should be placed in a warm, dry, dark, well-ventilated place. It may take up to 10 days for herbs to dry.

Hang ★ Dry

Fasten small bunches of herbs together with a rubber band. Hang upside down to dry (the herbs, not YOU, silly) — make sure there's plenty of room between the bundles for good air circulation. A clothes-drying rack makes an excellent dryer. Paper bags may be tied over the bundles to protect them from light and to catch falling dried leaves. This method might take up to 2 weeks.

Oven Drying ★

Place herbs in a single layer on flat, dry baking sheets. Small leaves may be dried right on the stem. Place in oven with door slightly ajar. Set oven temperature to lowest setting. Turn leaves on a regular basis. Drying might take 1 to 3 hours, depending on size of leaves and number of baking sheets.

MICROWAVING ★

Place a single layer of herbs on a double-thickness of paper toweling. Cover with a single layer of towel. Set timer for 2-3 minutes based on leaf size. Microwave on full power. Additional 30-second-shots may be needed to complete drying the leaves. Rotate herbs halfway through drying process. Don't overdry — if they turn to powder when touched, you went too far! Keep a notebook to record drying times for each herb to use a quick reference guide next time.

STORING HERBS ★

Keep in airtight containers in a cool, dry place. Glass & ceramic containers work well, as do metal ones. Paper and cardboard containers may absorb herbs' essential oils, so it's best to avoid those.

Check stored dried herbs for the first couple of weeks for moisture inside the jar — If left unchecked, mold may ruin all your hard work!

In March and in April
from morning to night
In sowing & seeding
good housewives delight.
To have in their garden
or some other plot;
to trim up their house &
to furnish their pot. — THOMAS TUSSER (1524-1580)
ENGLISH POET

Cooking with Herbs

KISS
THE
HERBAL
COOK
♥

GARDEN PATCH

POTATO SOUP

3 leeks, chopped
1 c. celery, chopped
½ c. onion, chopped
3 T. butter or margarine
4 c. raw potato, chopped

4 · 16 oz. cans chicken broth
2 t. salt
1 t. dried rosemary
⅛ t. white pepper
1 pint cream (2 cups)

In a large saucepan, sauté leeks, celery & onion
in butter. Add potatoes, broth & seasonings. Cover
with a lid and bring to a boil. Reduce heat &
simmer for 20-30 minutes. Just before serving,
stir in cream and heat through. Do not allow it
to boil. Garnish with chopped parsley or
watercress.

Zucchini and Tomato Sauté

a country friends' favorite side dish

- 2 T. onion, chopped
- 2 T. butter
- 4 medium zucchini, sliced
- 2 lg. tomatoes, peeled & chopped
- 2 T. red wine vinegar
- ½ t. dried basil leaves, crushed
- ¼ t. salt
- 1/8 t. pepper
- 2 t. sesame seeds

4 zucchini down, 74,123 to go...

In a large skillet, sauté onion in butter until tender. Add zucchini and tomatoes. Over low heat, cook 'til zucchini is tender-crisp. Add red wine vinegar and seasonings except for the sesame seeds. Cook 1-2 minutes more for flavors to blend. Place in a warm serving dish and sprinkle with sesame seeds.

Kitchen Tips
FROM KATE

A BAY LEAF PLACED IN FLOUR OR DRIED BEANS WILL HELP KEEP BUGS OUT.

... HANG SPRIGS OF BASIL TO DRIVE AWAY FLIES.
(APPETIZING, EH?)

Minty Melon Salad

so cool and refreshing!

- 1 c. water
- 3/4 c. sugar
- 3 T. fresh lime juice
- 1½ t. fresh mint, chopped
- 5 c. watermelon, cubed
- 3 c. cantaloupe, cubed
- 3 c. honeydew, cubed
- 2 c. nectarines, sliced
- 1 c. fresh blueberries

Combine water, sugar, lime juice & mint leaves in a saucepan. Bring to a boil. Stirring constantly, boil mixture for 2 minutes. Remove from heat, cover & cool completely. In a large bowl, combine fruit. Pour cooled syrup over fruit - stir 'til well blended. Cover & chill at least 2 hours. Stir occasionally to blend flavors. Drain liquid before serving. Garnish with fresh mint sprigs.

ABOUT MINT: IT IS ONE OF THE MOST INVASIVE OF HERBS AND WILL QUICKLY TAKE OVER YOUR GARDEN SPOT ~ SET IT IN A BOTTOMLESS POT SET IN THE GROUND OR GROW IT IN A CONTAINER.

MICE HATE THE SMELL OF MINT!

Summer Thyme Dressing

DELICIOUS OVER SLICED TOMATOES & CUCUMBERS, TOO!

2 T. white wine vinegar
½ c. vegetable oil
2 T. red onion, finely chopped
1 garlic clove, minced
2 T. fresh basil, chopped

2 t. fresh thyme, finely chopped
1 t. dry mustard
½ t. salt
¼ t. black pepper

Combine all ingredients in a jar with a tight-fitting lid. Shake until well-blended. Pour over salad greens and toss.

SAVORY GREEN BEAN MEDLEY

MY FAVORITE!

SAVORY & BEANS ARE A MATCH MADE IN HEAVEN!

1½ LB. FRESH GREEN BEANS, HALVED
1 MEDIUM ONION, CUT IN RINGS
¼ C. CELERY, SLICED
2 CARROTS, CUT IN STRIPS
½ t. SALT
2-3 T. FRESH SAVORY, MINCED <u>OR</u>
    2-3 t. DRIED SAVORY
⅛ t. PEPPER
1 C. WATER
3 T. BUTTER

"To get the best results you must talk to your vegetables."

— CHARLES, PRINCE OF WALES

See ~ We told you so! (Didn't we, sweetie?)

COMBINE ALL INGREDIENTS, EXCEPT BUTTER, IN LARGE SAUCEPAN — BRING TO BOIL. COVER AND REDUCE HEAT. SIMMER VEGETABLES FOR 5-10 MINUTES OR 'TIL TENDER. DRAIN. PLACE IN SERVING BOWL. MELT BUTTER IN A SMALL SKILLET — HEAT UNTIL IT JUST STARTS TO TURN BROWN. POUR OVER VEGETABLES AND SERVE.

16

THE Pizza Garden

...a great way to introduce herbs and gardening to children! Have them help you plant basil, oregano, marjoram and garlic, along with tomatoes, green peppers and onions.

Then enjoy...

Mary Elizabeth's Garden Pizza Sauce

QUICK and EASY TO PREPARE

6 OZ. CAN TOMATO PASTE

1 GARLIC CLOVE, MINCED

1 t. FRESH OREGANO LEAVES, CHOPPED OR ½ t. DRIED

1 t. FRESH BASIL LEAVES, CHOPPED OR ½ t. DRIED

¼ t. FRESH MARJORAM LEAVES, CHOPPED OR ⅛ t. DRIED

1 t. SUGAR

¼ c. WATER

Combine ingredients in a mixing bowl until well-blended. Spread on pizza dough and top with your favorite toppings.

Rose Geranium Cake

Basic White Cake never tasted so good!

8 ROSE GERANIUM LEAVES
2-LAYER WHITE CAKE MIX PLUS THE
  INGREDIENTS LISTED ON PACKAGE

GREASE & FLOUR THE SIDES OF 2 ROUND
CAKE PANS. CUT A WAX PAPER CIRCLE TO FIT
INSIDE BOTTOM OF PAN. LIGHTLY GREASE
WAX PAPER CIRCLE BEFORE PLACING INSIDE PAN.
LAY 4 LEAVES ON WAX PAPER BEFORE POURING IN
BATTER. PREPARE CAKE AS DESCRIBED ON MIX PACKAGE.
POUR BATTER OVER LEAVES IN PREPARED PANS. BAKE ACCORDING
TO PACKAGE INSTRUCTIONS. COOL IN PAN FOR 5-10 MINUTES.
INVERT PANS ONTO WIRE RACKS. REMOVE PANS & COOL. REMOVE
WAX PAPER CIRCLES.

Rose Petal Icing

1½ c. SUGAR	DASH OF SALT	¼ t. CREAM OF TARTAR
2 EGG WHITES	½ t. VANILLA	
5 T. COLD WATER	4 DROPS RED FOOD COLORING	

BEAT SUGAR, EGG WHITES, WATER, CREAM OF TARTAR & SALT
IN TOP OF DOUBLE BOILER UNTIL WELL BLENDED. PLACE OVER
BOILING WATER (UPPER PAN SHOULD NOT TOUCH WATER).
CONSTANTLY BEAT FOR 7 MINUTES ∿ STIFF PEAKS SHOULD
JUST BE STARTING TO FORM. DO NOT OVERCOOK! REMOVE PAN
FROM HEAT. ADD VANILLA & RED FOOD COLORING. CONTINUE
TO BEAT 'TIL ICING IS OF SPREADING CONSISTENCY ∿ ABOUT
2 MINUTES. FILL BETWEEN CAKE LAYERS WITH ICING, THEN
FROST CAKE. DECORATE WITH FRESH ROSE GERANIUM LEAVES
& EDIBLE FLOWERS IF YOU WISH.

In a garden, after a rainfall, you can faintly, yes, hear the breaking of new blooms. — TRUMAN CAPOTE

celebrate springtime with an

Herbal Tea Time

Set a table with pink and
yellow linens ... serve Rose
Geranium Cake and tall
glasses of minty ice tea on
your best white china. Pink geraniums
may grace the table's center.

Quick Herb Biscuits

— SHARE A BASKET-FULL WITH A COUNTRY FRIEND!

4 T. BUTTER OR MARGARINE
2 t. ONION, FINELY CHOPPED
1 t. DRIED DILL WEED
½ t. DRIED CHOPPED PARSLEY
1 10-OZ. TUBE REFRIGERATED BISCUITS

COMBINE BUTTER, ONION & HERBS IN SMALL SAUCEPAN. MELT OVER LOW HEAT. COOL SLIGHTLY. CUT BISCUITS IN HALF — THEY'LL LOOK LIKE A HALF-MOON. DIP EACH HALF IN BUTTER MIXTURE & PLACE IN SINGLE LAYER ON UNGREASED 9 INCH SQUARE BAKING DISH. DRIZZLE A LITTLE OF REMAINING BUTTER MIXTURE OVER BISCUITS. BAKE 8-10 MINUTES AT 450°.

MINE! ALL MINE!

Herb Butter

1 c. BUTTER
1 t. lemon Juice
1 T. freshly minced herbs

Allow butter to soften at room temperature. Beat butter & lemon juice until fluffy. Blend in minced herbs. Set aside for at least 1 hour to blend flavors.

★ For a very special look, chill butter and cut into shapes with cookie cutters. Add herb sprigs or edible flowers to decorate the butter pats!

SOME SUGGESTED HERBS FOR BUTTER:

GARLIC
CHIVES
DILL
MINT
ROSEMARY
BASIL
THYME
SAVORY
TARRAGON
PARSLEY
ONION
OREGANO
…experiment!

country Friends Fresh,

CULINARY HERB WREATH

YOU WILL NEED:
- 1 COAT HANGER
- 22-GAUGE FLORIST WIRE
- BUNCHES OF FRESH HERBS *
- FLORIST TAPE

Remove top of coat hanger with wire cutters. Shape into circle or heart by using florist tape to wrap ends together securely and tightly.

Wire bunches of herbs to the wire wreath frame with florist wire. Place each new bunch over the stems of the previously-wired herbs, and continue this layering process all around the wreath. Secure end of wire, and make loop at top for hanging.

* As fresh herbs dry, the bundles will shrink in size, so pack as many bunches on the wreath as you can to avoid bare spots. Some great culinary herbs are: BASIL • THYME • BAY LEAVES • DILL • GARLIC HEADS • SAGE • MARJORAM • OREGANO • MINT • SAVORY • CHERVIL • ROSEMARY

Cultivate the garden for the nose, and the eyes will take care of themselves.
—ROBERT LOUIS STEVENSON

Lemon Verbena Honey

1 C. HONEY
1 SPRIG OR SEVERAL LEAVES OF FRESH LEMON VERBENA

HEAT HONEY OVER LOW HEAT. PLACE HERBS IN CLEAN JAR—POUR WARM HONEY IN. SEAL & AGE FOR AT LEAST 1 WEEK.

SPICY TEX*MEX CHICKEN

¡AY CARÁMBA! COLORFUL and DELICIOUS!

6 boneless, skinless chicken breast halves
2 T. fresh lime juice
½ t. salt
¼ t. ground red pepper
⅓ c. olive oil
1 med. red onion, chopped
1 sm. red pepper, chopped
1 sm. yellow pepper, chopped
1 clove garlic, minced
¼ c. plus 2 T. fresh cilantro, chopped
6-8 ripe tomatoes, sliced
2 c. Monterey jack cheese, shredded
cilantro sprigs for garnish
lime slices for garnish

Place chicken breast halves between wax paper ~ pound 'til slightly flat. In small bowl, combine lime juice, salt & red pepper. Add chicken to marinade ~ toss to coat. Let stand in marinade for 10-12 minutes. In large skillet, heat half of olive oil over medium heat. Sauté chicken 'til lightly browned on both sides. Remove from pan. Pour in remaining olive oil ~ heat. Sauté onions, peppers & garlic 'til tender-crisp ~ about 4-5 minutes. Remove pan from heat and add cilantro. Mix well.

Cover bottom of baking dish with ⅔s of sliced tomatoes. Layer half of onion-pepper mixture over tomato slices. Sprinkle with a bit more than just 1 cup of cheese. Place chicken on next in a single layer. Top with more tomato slices then more onion-pepper mixture. Bake for 15-25 minutes at 400° or 'til chicken is tender. Sprinkle on remaining cheese and return to oven 'til cheese is melted. Garnish with cilantro & lime slices.

Herbs for the Bath

You need...
Soothing Oatmeal Bath
...PAMPER YOURSELF AFTER A STRESSFUL DAY!

- 2 c. OATMEAL
- 1 c. CORN MEAL
- ½ c. DRIED ROSEMARY
- 1 c. LAVENDER FLOWERS
- ½ c. BAKING SODA
- ¼ c. POWDERED MILK

PULVERIZE OATMEAL IN FOOD PROCESSOR. ADD CORN MEAL & PROCESS AGAIN. ADD REMAINING INGREDIENTS & PROCESS 'TIL WELL-BLENDED. FILL SMALL MUSLIN BAGS WITH MIXTURE (TO KEEP FRESH, STORE IN TINS OR JARS.) PLACE UNDER FAUCET.

Lavender Bath Salts

- ½ c. Lemon Thyme, dried
- 1 c. Lavender flowers, dried
- 1 c. Baking Soda
- 1 c. epsom salts

Place all ingredients in a jar with a tight-fitting lid. Shake to mix well. Keep jar tightly closed to keep out moisture. Place 2-3 tablespoons in a muslin bath bag and place under running water.

Herbal Bath Gifts

are easy to make and wonderful to give. You can decorate the muslin bags with rubber stamps in herb or garden designs before filling... then simply tie closed with a string or ribbon long enough to hang from faucet. The bag can also be used as a bath mitt.

aaaahh

Herbal Gifts

KATE'S OH·SO·EASY FIREPLACE BUNDLES

...a thoughtful & fragrant gift for a housewarming!

It's simple — after you have harvested all your herbs, save the stems & clippings & extra pieces. Tie them all together in a bundle with raffia and put them in a bushel basket — the bundles may be tossed on a fire and their scents will fill the air!

HOLLY'S CATNIP PURSES

Dry catnip and crush it into small pieces. Cut out colorful felt shapes. Stitch 3 sides closed, and fill with pulverized catnip. Stitch opening closed. Give to your favorite feline country friend!

MARY ELIZABETH'S SWEET DREAMS PILLOW

Collect & dry sweet-smelling herbs & flowers, such as lavender, lemon balm, thyme, rosemary & chamomile. Place dried material, a teaspoon of ground orange or lemon peel and a tablespoon of orris root in a tightly-sealed jar. Keep in a dark spot for 10 days, then before using, add a few drops of essential oil — perhaps lavender. Sew a small pillowcase out of lightly-woven cotton homespun or calico, leaving one side open. Fill with the potpourri you've made, then stitch shut. This fragrant little pillow may be placed under a regular bed pillow — its lovely fragrance will lull you into dreamland!

GARDENER'S DELIGHT

Buy a pair of canvas garden gloves. Use craft paints to decorate the glove with a friend's name, and then fill the glove with an herb-scented potpourri. Stitch glove opening closed. Place in a clay pot with packages of herb seeds.

There's rosemary, that's for remembrance...

shakespeare

KICK OFF YOUR SHOES

A FUN LITTLE IDEA FOR YOUR GARDEN

❀ RAID THE BACK OF YOUR SON'S CLOSET FOR AN OLD PAIR OF HIGH TOP SNEAKERS ～OR～ AN ANCIENT PAIR OF WORK BOOTS, GARDEN CLOGS, ETC... THE MORE RIPPED & BEAT-UP THE BETTER!

❀ IN THE DESIRED LOCATION, MAKE AN INDENTATION IN THE GROUND THE SIZE OF THE SHOES. YOU MIGHT WANT TO PLACE ONE SHOE UPRIGHT & THE OTHER LYING ON ITS SIDE. FILL IN WITH A LITTLE DIRT AROUND SHOES TO ANCHOR.

❀ NOW - FILL THE SHOES WITH SOIL ～PACK IT IN THERE!

GROW BIG POTTING SOIL

❀ HERE'S THE **FUN** PART : PLANT THE SHOES FULL OF HERBS! PLANTS LIKE CORSICAN MINT, WOOLY OR CREEPING THYME, HEN-AND-CHICKS ARE GREAT TO USE. YOU CAN PUT THEM COMING OUT THE HOLES IN THE SHOES AS WELL AS OUT OF THE TOPS! (YOU MIGHT PULL THE SHOE TONGUES DOWN AND LOOSEN THE LACES TO GIVE MORE PLANTING ROOM). WATER THOROUGHLY AND ENJOY! AS PLANTS FILL IN, IT APPEARS THE GARDEN IS TAKING OVER AN OLD PAIR OF FORGOTTEN SHOES.

A SWEET IDEA: PLANT A PAIR OF LITTLE GIRL'S MARYJANES FOR YOUR PORCH.

Herbal Notecards

Dear friend,
What a great way to share the beauty of the garden! love, Holly

You will need:

- WRITING PAPER (70-LB. WEIGHT) OR A 5½" × 7½" PIECE OF DECORATIVE RICE PAPER
- 4" × 6" ENVELOPES (RECYCLED, NATURAL OR KRAFT PAPER LOOKS NEAT)
- SPRIGS, LEAVES OR FLOWERS OF HERBS
- NEWSPAPER
- HEAVY BOOKS
- WHITE CRAFT GLUE
- WAX PAPER
- TOOTHPICKS
- SMALL PAINT BRUSH

Select herbs just as you would for any drying process. For notecards, select smaller, delicate sprigs, leaves or petals.

Layer herbs between sheets of newspaper to press ~ allow plenty of room between herbs. Place heavy books on top of newspaper. It may take 1 to 2 weeks for herbs to dry & be flattened, depending on quantity of layers & type of herbs.

Fold writing paper in half to form 3¾" × 5½" card.

Lay dried herbs (with best side down) on wax paper. Using toothpick or small paint brush, apply white craft glue. Gently pick up and place in desired location on front of card. Let set for about 5 minutes. Cover with clean piece of wax paper ~ set a heavy book on top for about 15 minutes. Remove book & wax paper. Allow glue to dry completely.

Package several notecards & envelopes together with a raffia bow. Glue a dried herb sprig to the bow for a beautiful finishing touch, OR,

write to a special friend on one! What a wonderful thing to find in your mailbox!

Old Friends & Old Shoes feel best.
— old proverb

Herbal Garden Seat

#1 OK— measure the seat opening, length by width. Now double those measurements. (For example, if seat opening is 14" x 12", cut the mesh screen 28" x 24".)

#2 Lay screen over seat opening — gently push it through until a fairly deep pouch or cavity is formed. Staple mesh to chair around top of opening — trim away any excess.

#3 Line pouch with sheets of sphagnum moss, with green mossy side touching the screen.

#4 Doublecheck! Be sure the mesh screen is completely covered by moss. (If moss is hard to work with, soak it in a little water to make it more pliable.)

#5 Fill pouch with potting soil. SOIL

Plant herbs in chair seat pouch. Place taller herbs to the back, and low-growing or creeping plants more to the front and sides.

#7 Water Thoroughly.

#8 Place your garden seat in the herb garden, or by the porch or walkway where you can enjoy it!

YOU DID IT!

Some little extras
IF YOU FEEL PARTICULARLY ARTSY ....

add a bit of whimsy with a piece of fungus for a fairy chair ♥ a GARDEN SIGN in among the herbs ♥ a little green toad under the chair ♥ paint a garden verse on the slats of the chair.

Peace

A GARDEN is a Lovesome thing, God wot!

– Thomas Edward Brown

ALL THAT IN THIS DELIGHTFUL GARDEN GROWS, SHOULD HAPPY BE AND HAVE IMMORTAL BLISS. ～ edmund spenser

THE HERBS OF CHRISTMAS

Chamomile, horehound, lavender, rosemary, thyme, bedstraw & sweet woodruff are the herbs of Christmas. Legend has it that Mary hung her wash to dry on lavender & rosemary plants. The swaddling clothes of Baby Jesus gave the scentless lavender plant its wonderful fragrance. It is also said that Mary's cloak changed the white rosemary blossoms blue. The other herbs are thought to be mixed with the straw in the manger.

Add fresh or dried sprigs of the Christmas herbs to your manger — put small pots of fresh rosemary or lavender potpourri around the nativity set.

what an IDEA!

...AN HERBAL INSPIRATION!

SPRINKLE ROSEMARY LEAVES IN YOUR CHRISTMAS CARD or GET-WELL CARD ENVELOPES to say "Remember Me."

TAKE AN EARLY A.M. WALK IN THE HERB GARDEN TO APPRECIATE THEM AT THEIR FRAGRANCE PEAK. Take along a good book and read a bit in the peace and quiet.

KEEP OLD PHONE BOOKS & DIRECTORIES TO STORE PRESSED HERBS & FLOWERS. LAYER THEM BETWEEN THE PAGES — FILE THE PRESSED HERBS ALPHABETICALLY FOR EASY REFERENCE IF YOU ARE SO INCLINED.

YELLOW PAGES

– I LIKE THIS IDEA FROM A RECYCLING POINT OF VIEW BUT I THINK IF ONE HAS TIME TO FILE ONE'S HERBS ALPHABETICALLY, ONE NEEDS TO FIND A HOBBY. QUICKLY.

Some
Good
Old-
Fashioned
Herbal
Folklore
& Fable

from
Kate's
Garden

a scarecrow in red will keep herbs in the bed.

RESEARCH HAS
SHOWN SCARLET
TO BE THE MOST
EFFECTIVE COLOR
FOR SCARING
AWAY BIRDS
FROM THE
GARDEN.

plant a plot of Southernwood to find a love who's true & good.

Southernwood was considered an aphrodisiac and was sometimes called "LAD'S LOVE" in earlier times.

Grow summer savory for speedy relief from a wasp's sting—just rub on a leaf!

A swarm of bees in May is worth a load of Hay.

RABBITS HATE ONIONS~
PLANT SOME TO PROTECT
YOUR GARDEN! THEY
LOVE DILL ~ PLANT IT
AS A DIVERSION.

When snails climb up a blade of grass, rainy skies will come to pass.

Thyme, hyssop & sage are said to deter snails.

Wear a sprig of rosemary to guard thee against plague & to avert the evil eye.

DOGS DETEST RUE — plant some by the garden gate to keep Spotty out.

KATE'S HERBAL TRIVIA

One of the charms of herbs lies in their common names; these are some of my favorite "folk" names that herbs have gained in times past~

Heartsease
also known as call-me-to-you, love in idleness

Dandelion
lion's teeth, fairy clock

Foxglove
dead men's bells, bloody fingers, fairy caps

Tarragon little dragon

Yarrow
nosebleed, carpenter's weed

Meadowsweet
Queen of the Meadows

Lady's Mantle
Bear's foot, nine hooks

Horsetail
Bottlebrush, paddock pipes

31

Herbs

Garden shed

I like to think of old gardeners pottering their life·time away in green baize aprons, straw hats, a twist of raffia behind their ears, and a Nannie-like intimacy with the plants in their care. —VITA SACKVILLE-WEST